# SLIME-INATORS
## & Other Slippery Tricksters

# POISON SLIMERS

## POISON DART FROGS, SEA CUCUMBERS, AND MORE

by Ellen Lawrence

**Consultants:**
**David R. Bellwood,** James Cook University, Queensland, Australia
**Alexander Bär,** Leipzig University, Leipzig, Germany
**Kyle Summers,** East Carolina University, Greenville, North Carolina

# BEARPORT
### PUBLISHING

New York, New York

**Credits**

Cover, © Brandon Alms/Shutterstock; 4, © Neil Bowman/FLPA; 5, © Thomas Marent/Minden Pictures/FLPA; 6BL, © schankz/Shutterstock; 6TR, © Cyril Papot/Shutterstock; 6BR, © Dirk Ercken/Shutterstock; 7, © Mark Moffett/Minden Pictures/FLPA; 8, © blickwinkel/Alamy; 9, © George Grall/Getty Images; 10T, © Baer, A. et al., Nature Communications (2017); 10B, © Dr. Morley Read/Shutterstock; 11, © FLPA/Alamy; 12, © Yongkiet Jitwattanatam/Shutterstock; 13, © Mark Moffett/Minden Pictures/FLPA; 14T, © John A. Andersen/Shutterstock; 14B, © Gino Santa Maria/Shutterstock; 15, © Gerard Soury/Getty Images; 16, © cbimages/Alamy; 17, © age fotostock/Alamy; 18T, © Lukiyanova Natalia Frenta/Shutterstock; 18B, © David Havel/Shutterstock; 19, © Levent Konuk/Shutterstock; 20T, © Studio II/Shutterstock; 20B, © sciencepics/Shutterstock; 21, © Dennis Kunkel Microscopy/Science Photo Library; 22TL, © Ruth Owen Books; 22BL, © Bret Skagerberg/Shutterstock; 22R, © jarabee123/Shutterstock; 23TL, © Emanuele Biggi/FLPA; 23TC, © sciencepics/Shutterstock; 23TR, © Suwan Wanawattanawong/Shutterstock; 23BL, © wildestanimal/Shutterstock; 23BC, © saraporn/Shutterstock; 23BR, © Dirk Ercken/Shutterstock.

Publisher: Kenn Goin
Senior Editor: Joyce Tavolacci
Creative Director: Spencer Brinker
Photo Researcher: Ruth Owen Books

*Library of Congress Cataloging-in-Publication Data*

Names: Lawrence, Ellen, 1967– author.
Title: Poison slimers : poison dart frogs, sea cucumbers & more / by Ellen
   Lawrence.
Description: New York, New York : Bearport Publishing, [2019] | Series:
   Slime-inators & other slippery tricksters | Includes
   bibliographical references and index.
Identifiers: LCCN 2018018543 (print) | LCCN 2018020350 (ebook) |
   ISBN 9781684027446 (ebook) | ISBN 9781684026982 (library)
Subjects: LCSH: Dendrobatidae—Juvenile literature. | Sea cucumbers—Juvenile
   literature. | Poisonous animals—Juvenile literature.
Classification: LCC QL668.E233 (ebook) | LCC QL668.E233 L39 2019 (print) |
   DDC 597.8/77—dc23
LC record available at https://lccn.loc.gov/2018018543

For more information, write to Bearport Publishing Company, Inc., 45 West 21st Street, Suite 3B, New York, New York 10010. Printed in the United States of America.

10 9 8 7 6 5 4 3 2 1

# Contents

# Slimy and Deadly

A tiny yellow frog is climbing on a leafy tree in a rain forest.

Suddenly, a large black bird lands on a nearby branch.

Is the frog about to become the bird's next meal? Think again!

The yellow creature is a poison dart frog, and its body is covered with **toxic** slime.

The bird knows that eating the slimy frog will mean instant death!

a black caracara bird

# Killer Slime!

There are many kinds of poison frogs.

If a **predator** tries to eat one of these frogs, it will become paralyzed.

The frog's poisonous slime will make it impossible for the predator to move.

Poison frogs get their poison from the foods they eat.

They feed on toxic ants and beetles and store the poison inside their bodies.

blue poison frog

strawberry poison frog

A poison frog's colorful skin tells its enemies that it's dangerous to eat. How do animals learn that a frog's bright colors mean danger?
(The answer is on page 24.)

Native people who live in the rain forest wipe poison from golden poison dart frog's skin and put it on the tips of darts. Then, the darts are used for hunting. This is how the frogs got their name!

golden poison dart frog

dart

# A Sticky Salamander

Other animals use slime as a defense, too.

A northern slimy salamander can make a gluelike slime.

If a predator comes close, the salamander lashes its long tail from side to side.

If the enemy tries to attack, it gets a mouthful of sticky slime.

The slime is so gooey, it causes the predator's jaws to stick together!

Northern slimy salamanders live in forests. They spend their days hiding under rotting leaves and logs. At night, they hunt for small animals, such as insects and worms.

slimy skin

northern slimy salamander

long tail

# Jets of Slime

If an animal called a velvet worm is under attack, it blasts its enemy with two slime jets!

At first, the strands of slime are soft and sticky.

However, the goo soon turns rock-hard, and the worm's attacker can't escape.

A velvet worm also uses its slime jets to capture insects, spiders, and centipedes to eat.

glands

The slime comes from glands on either side of a velvet worm's head.

velvet worm

velvet worm

A velvet worm isn't actually a type of worm—it just looks like one! It belongs to a group of animals known as onychophorans (on-i-KOF-er-uhns).

velvet worm slime

a cockroach trapped in clear, sticky slime

How do you think an animal might use sticky, toxic slime as a defense?

# A Gooey Explosion

Creatures called exploding carpenter ants kill their enemies in a horrifying way.

Sometimes, an enemy ant tries to steal a carpenter ant's food.

When this happens, the ant grabs the enemy with its jaws.

Then, it "explodes," covering its enemy with toxic, yellow slime!

The slime explosion kills both the carpenter ant and the attacker.

ant jaws

To create an explosion, the carpenter ant twists and squeezes its lower body until it bursts. Then, its enemy gets splattered with toxic slime.

attacking ant

exploding carpenter ant

13

# Underwater Attack

Some poison slimers live in the ocean.

A trunkfish may be small, but it can kill a big predator.

If a shark chases the little fish, poisonous slime oozes from the fish's skin.

The cloud of toxic slime spreads through the water.

If the shark swallows the slimy water, it will die!

trunkfish

blacktip reef sharks

a trunkfish
looking for food

Trunkfish feed on
small animals, such as
shrimp and worms, that hide
in sand. To uncover a meal,
a trunkfish shoots a jet of
water from its mouth
into the sand.

sand blasted
by jets of water

15

# A Cucumber Fights Back

A sea cucumber is a slow-moving ocean animal—but it isn't an easy meal to catch.

If a predator tries to bite it, the cucumber shoots slimy strings from its backside!

The spaghetti-like, sticky strings wrap around the attacker's body.

As the predator tries to untangle itself, the sea cucumber makes its escape.

a sea cucumber sending out slimy strings

sea cucumber

When attacked, some types of sea cucumbers also release deadly poison into the water.

a black sea cucumber defending itself

a crab tangled in slimy strings

# Slime for Protection

A clownfish uses slime for protection.

If a predator attacks, a clownfish hides among the **tentacles** of a sea anemone.

Watch out! The anemone's tentacles can deliver a deadly sting.

Why don't the stinging tentacles hurt the tiny clownfish?

The clownfish is covered with a special slime that protects its body!

clownfish

sea anemone

A clownfish and a sea anemone are good partners. The fish gets protection from the anemone. In return, the fish keeps the anemone clean by eating algae and leftover food from the anemone's tentacles.

tentacles

Your body produces a type of protective slime, too. What do you think it is and how does it protect you?

# In Your Nose!

It's not just wild animals that defend themselves with slime—humans do, too!

The air you breathe goes into your **lungs**.

This air contains germs and dirt that can harm your body.

Your nose produces a thick, sticky **mucus** that traps these invaders before they enter your lungs.

Mucus helps protect your body every day!

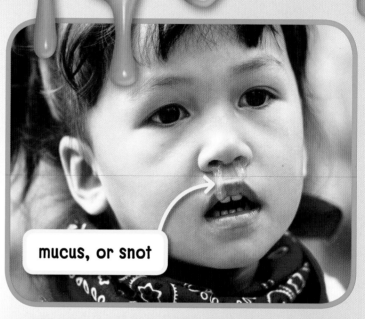

mucus, or snot

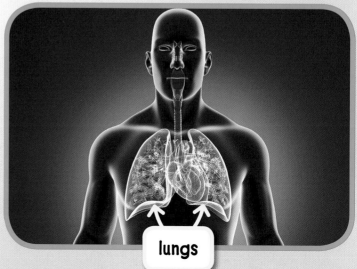

lungs

a nose hair

Each day,
a person's nose
produces about
2 pints (1 liter)
of mucus!

mucus

a grain of pollen
from a plant
trapped in mucus

This picture shows mucus
inside a person's nose, as seen
under a powerful microscope.

# Science Lab

## Let's Make Slime!

The animals in this book make different kinds of slime. Get ready to make and investigate your own slime!

1. In a bowl, mix together the warm water and baking soda until the baking soda has dissolved.

2. Add the glue to the bowl and mix well.

3. Add a small amount of food coloring or glitter if you like.

4. Next, add the contact lens solution one tablespoon at a time, stirring until the slime forms.

5. Take the slime out of the bowl and knead it with your hands until it forms a firm shape.

**You will need:**
- A bowl
- A spoon for mixing
- ¼ cup warm water
- ½ teaspoon baking soda
- 5 fluid ounces clear Elmer's glue
- Food coloring or glitter
- Up to 3 tablespoons contact lens solution

## Slime Investigation

Water pours easily because it's a liquid and flows. Peanut butter is a solid and doesn't usually pour at all. Hold your blob of slime and let it pour, or ooze, from your fingers.

- **How easily does your slime pour? Is it more like water, peanut butter, or something else?**

Put a small blob of slime in the freezer overnight. What do you think will happen to it? Write down your prediction in a notebook.

- **Did your prediction match what happened?**

A sea cucumber makes slimy threads.

- **How would you make long, sticky threads with your slime?**

# Science Words

**glands** (GLANDZ)  body parts that produce chemicals

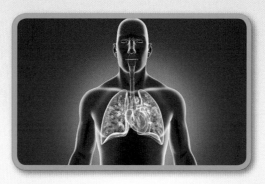

**lungs** (LUHNGZ)  body parts in the chest that are used for breathing

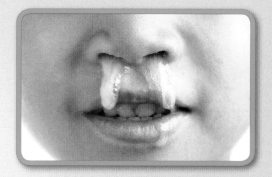

**mucus** (MYOO-kuhss) a thick, sticky liquid made by the body

**predator** (PRED-uh-tur) an animal that hunts other animals for food

**tentacles** (TEN-tuh-kuhlz) long body parts used by some animals for moving, feeling, or grasping

**toxic** (TOK-sik)  poisonous

# Index

# Read More

Dussling, Jennifer. *Deadly Poison Dart Frogs (Gross-Out Defenses).* New York: Bearport (2009).

Hirsch, Rebecca E. *Exploding Ants and Other Amazing Defenses (Animal Superpowers).* Minneapolis, MN: Lerner (2017).

Rake, Jody S. *Sea Cucumbers (Faceless, Spineless, and Brainless Ocean Animals).* North Mankato, MN: Capstone (2017).

# Learn More Online

To learn more about poison slimers, visit
**www.bearportpublishing.com/Slime-inators**

# About the Author

Ellen Lawrence lives in the United Kingdom. Her favorite books to write are those about nature and animals. In fact, the first book Ellen bought for herself when she was six years old was the story of a gorilla named Patty Cake that was born in New York's Central Park Zoo.

# Answer for Page 7

A predator might get a tiny taste of a poison dart frog and become very ill. The predator will remember that the colorful frog was harmful and keep away from it in the future. Other animals are born knowing that bright colors mean danger. This type of knowledge is called "instinctual."